Animal
Colors
and More

for Zach xx

Animal Colors

and More

by Katie Viggers

Brooklyn, NY

dark **brown**

yakkity yak

brown bear

light **brown**

camel

lion

The Grays

gray squirrel

African elephant

hippopotamus

koala bear

shoebill

gray wolf

pink

The six types of flamingo

American

Andean

lesser

james's

Chilean

greater

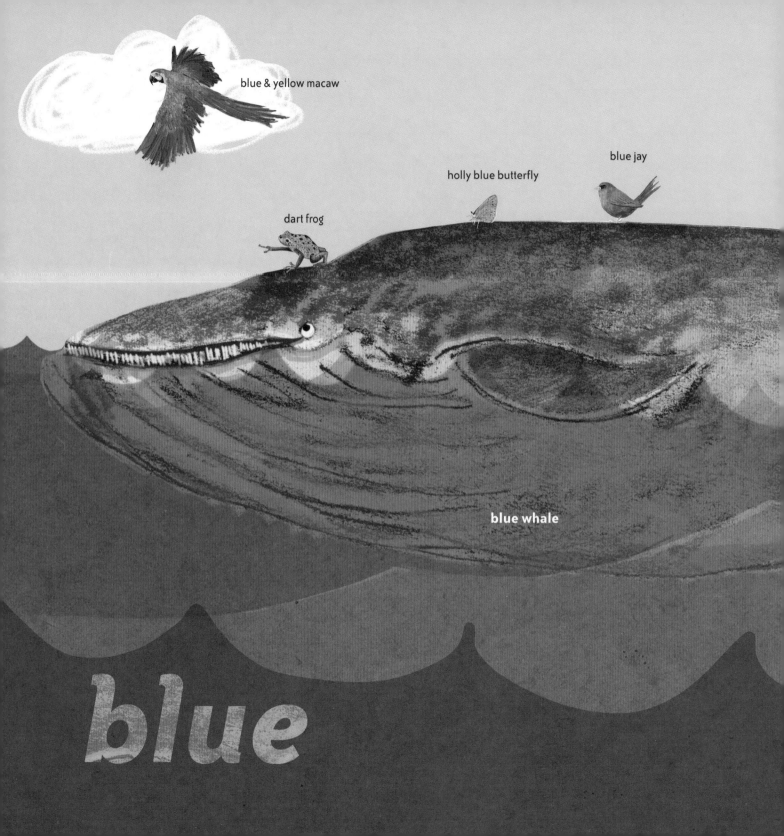

blue & yellow macaw

blue jay

holly blue butterfly

dart frog

blue whale

blue

dolphin

regal tang

red

strawberry
dart frog

scarlet ibis

cardinal

tomato frog

red

only by name, not by color

they should be on the next page really.......

red squirrel

red panda

red fox

red kangaroo

orange

cock-of-the-rock

golden lion tamarin

orangutan

baby
orangutan
and his pet
goldfish

Mostly White

swan

East Friesian sheep

mouse

Arctic hare

weasel

polar bear

seagull

Some animals have

spots

peacock   helmeted guineafowl

spot the difference

leopard

cheetah

black

black
squirrell

Tazmainian devil

crow

black bear
(American)

gorilla

blackberry
pie

Green

ring necked parrakeet

Can you
find the
grass snake
and the
grasshopper?

chameleon

honeycreepers

female

male

iguana

some animals are

stripy

bongo

okapi

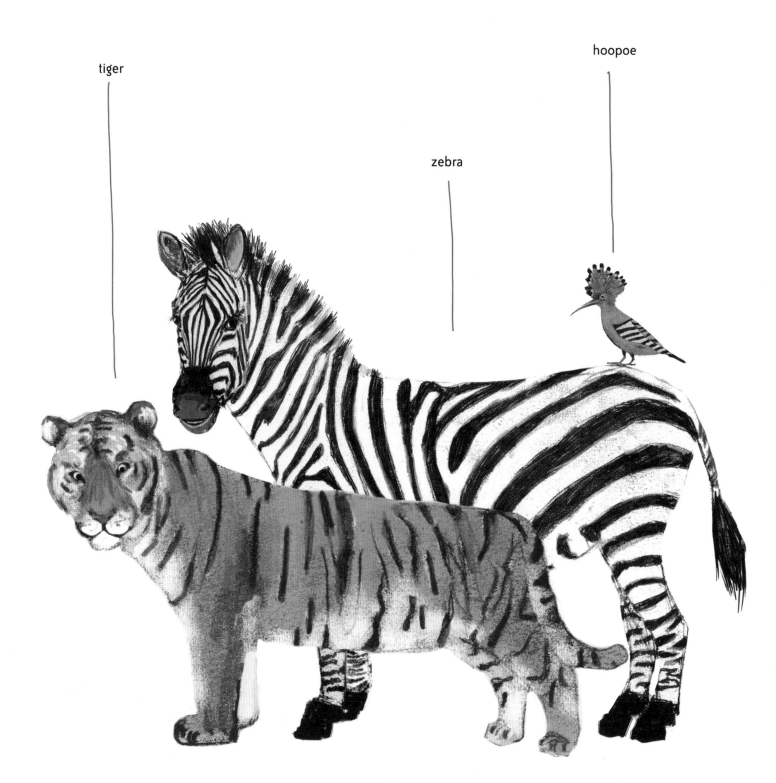

tiger

zebra

hoopoe

yellow

duckling

duckling

duckling

duckling

duckling

rubber duck

duckling

duckling

duckling

purple

Admittedly only one of these is actually purple.

Can you guess which one?

East Friesian sheep

chameleon

purple emperor

polar bear

Also from Katie Viggers:

An Animal A-Z book

New Edition

An Animal Counting Book

1 to 20
Animals Aplenty

by Katie Viggers

Animal Colors and More

Published by POW!
a division of powerHouse Packaging & Supply, Inc.
32 Adams Street, Brooklyn, NY 11201-1021
info@powkidsbooks.com • www.powkidsbooks.com
www.powerHouseBooks.com • www.powerHousePackaging.com

Library of Congress Control Number: 2016953553

ISBN: 978-1-57687-829-3

10 9 8 7 6 5 4 3 2 1

Printed in Malaysia

Can you name
all the animals?